SIMPLE STARTS

For Business Builders

The Dynamic Life Group.com

LEADING WITH INTENTION IN FREEDOM & EMPOWERMENT

Table of Contents

Step 1: Sign up for Essential Rewards 5

Step 2: Purchase Reference Material. 8

Step 3: Let's Start Sharing! 8

Step 4: Follow Up 16

Step 5: Structure Your Organization 18

Step 6: Duplicate! 20

Step 7: Building to Silver 24

Reference Materials & Business Building Tools 32

Important Links 32

MLM Business Based 33

Daily OGV & New Member Tracker 34

Upline Contact Info 35

© Dana Bailey, All Rights Reserved 2016

FOR I AM ABOUT TO DO SOMETHING NEW.

SEE, I HAVE ALREADY BEGUN!

DO YOU NOT SEE IT?

I WILL MAKE A PATHWAY THROUGH THE WILDERNESS.

I WILL CREATE RIVERS IN THE DRY WASTELAND.

ISAIAH 43:19 (NLT)

SIMPLE START GUIDE

This book is meant to be a simple guide to help you quickly jump start your Young Living experience. We hope this helps you not only make the most of your own YL membership, but also help others to do the same. There are many ways to build a business. This booklet is giving you seven simple steps and ideas that we have used. These steps can be tweaked to fit your own personal timeline, lifestyle, goals and situation. Check off the steps as you complete each one along the way on your journey to success. Building a business is never easy, but it doesn't have to be complicated. Follow these seven simple steps and you will be on your way to creating a forever income. If you need help or have any questions, please do not hesitate to reach out to your upline support team. Your upline are here to help you!

If you already have team members, wanting to know how to share YL with others, use this book your members and help them get off to a simple, but quick start in building their Young Living business.

"Success is nothing more than a few simple disciplines, practiced every day."
Jim Rohn

Step 1: Sign up for Essential Rewards

Essential Rewards is YL's monthly auto-ship program. This is an easy decision when you realize what a great benefit this will be to you. In order for you to earn bonuses, you will need to place a monthly order of at least 50PV. To receive unilevel commission you need to place an order of at least 100PV. In the beginning, your checks will mostly be made up of bonuses. As your organization grows you will begin earning unilevel commission.

Once you sign up your first member, make sure you are maximizing the compensation plan to the fullest.

- ✓ Order at least 50PV in months 1-3
- ✓ Order at least 100 PV from month 4 onward.

UPGRADE YOUR REWARDS
Check out the changes to our Essential Rewards program!

The exciting enhancements to the Essential Rewards program go live September 1, 2016! ER Members will now not only enjoy an increased percentage of their orders back in points, but also can earn fabulous Loyalty Gifts for consistently ordering* each month. Here are the points and gifts from the US market:

Points
Months 1-3 – 10% of order PV back in points
Months 4-24 – 20% of order PV back in points
Months 25+ – 25% of order PV back in points

Loyalty Gifts
After 3 months of consecutive orders - Peppermint Vitality Oil, 5ml
After 6 months of consecutive orders - Thieves Oil Blend, 5ml
After 9 months of consecutive orders - Breathe Again Roll-On, 10ml
After 12 months of consecutive orders - Exclusive Loyalty Oil Blend formulated by Gary
For those outside the US, please refer to your home market for more details on the program.

*Minimum market ER PV requirements must be met for order to count as consecutive

© Dana Bailey, All Rights Reserved 2016

Step 2: Purchase Reference Material.

This step is really important because your reference material will help you educate yourself on the products and how you can use them. We want all of our members to have reference material, but if you are going to be talking about the products to other people you really need to have it. You need to educate yourself on the products you will be helping others to begin using. We are not trying to be the experts, but we do need to be educated. We can avoid being the experts when we are able to direct people to 3rd party resources.

It is a blessing to have many resources to assist us in learning how to use our essential oils. If you are not sure what resources to start with, talk to your closest upline leader. They are here to help you.

In the resource section of this guide are links to help you find various resource materials.

"If you are using essential oils, you need to have some reference materials. There is so much to these oils and the reference books help me so much in learning how to use them. If it weren't for my reference materials I would call my team leader all the time asking questions."
Dynamic LIFE Group team member

Step 3: Let's Start Sharing!

Who can you share with? The obvious place to start is with people you know. Young Living keeps relationships as the priority, not just selling a product. We want to find better health and wellness not just better products.

Gary Young says, "*Just be a friend*". Be real and genuine with others. People know if you care about them or just care about selling a product. Once your friends realize you genuinely care about them they will be more open to listen to you share how great the products are. I have helped many friends get their own membership with Young Living who told me they signed up with me because they trusted me and knew I would help them. This is a relationship based business!

> *Think of people in your life…*
>
> - *Interested in natural health & wellness*
> - *Entrepreneurs*
> - *Interested in earning extra income.*
> - *With influence*

Your family and your love must be cultivated like a garden. Time, effort, and imagination must be summoned constantly to keep any relationship flourishing and growing." Jim Rohn

---

Be genuine. People can spot a fake a mile away & if you are only after them for their YL Membership, they will know it.

I think it is important to tell you that how you share Young Living with someone when they join is most likely how they will share Young Living with others. Doing things in a way that others can also do is called being duplicable. We will talk more about this soon. So, keep that in mind. Your new member will learn how to duplicate what you do from the very beginning.

Start your list. You need to begin thinking of people you want to introduce Young Living products to. On page 10, begin our list of names of people you know that you think would be interested. It's simply a starting place.

Recognizing Circles of Relationships

It naturally happens, we create circles of relationships in our lives. We have friends from school, work, family, playgroups… Recognizing these circles can help you as you share with your friends to create a team of people who are already close and now will have something else in common…a love for essential oils.

Identify below 7 circles of relationships that you have already. This will help when it is time to start inviting people to your first essential oils class.

1. _____
2. _____
3. _____
4. _____
5. _____
6. _____
7. _____

© Dana Bailey, All Rights Reserved 2016

You will need 7 "legs" to grow to Royal Crown Diamond. Focusing on 7 circles of relationships will help you to organize your team from the beginning into groups of people who already know each other.

Always Be Prepared!

Be ready to take advantage of the natural opportunities to share Young Living with others. Carry your favorite oils in your purse or bag. Keep brochures or fliers of the Premium Starter Kit in your car. It is guaranteed that when your friends see you using oils with your kids or on yourself, they are going to be curious and most often will begin asking questions. This is a great way to naturally introduce someone to the world of essential oils.

Make a list of places you go on a regular basis.

_____

_____

_____

_____

_____

_____

Time to Share!

The key to any successful business is action! Your first event is critical in getting your business off to a strong start. You can host this in your home, or somewhere else. This is your way of showing your friends what you are doing and giving them an opportunity to get involved with you.

Launch Date: _____

Location: _____

Send this to your upline leader & let her know so that she can continue to encourage you & cheer you on.

For your launch event, be sure to invite people from each of the 7 circles of relationships you identified earlier. The invitation is just as important as the event. If we don't invite, no one will come. Here is an invitation process that I learned from Vicki Opfer (Royal Crown Diamond) and together with my upline leader we found this to be a very effective way of creating a fun, and interesting environment of friends at our events.

> Do you have friends long distance you want to share with? Facebook Classes, Skype or other online resources make that possible!

Invite at least 2 people from each of your 7 circles (if they are local to you). Ask those you invite to bring at least 2 friends with them. You don't have to be the only one inviting people to your event. When your friends bring friends that extends your reach a great deal.

When you invite people to your launch event, let those who cannot attend know when your next event is. If they still can't come, but are interested, schedule a time to meet with them one on one. This is a fantastic way to introduce someone in a very personal way to Young Living products.

© Dana Bailey, All Rights Reserved 2016

Book Classes

The goal of the launch event is to engage your friends by having them host classes for you to teach or team teach with your leader. The goal is to get one class booked in each group at your launch. So have your calendar ready to fill up. A full calendar is one of the secrets to growing your team quickly.

Class Booking Tips

If you have a difficult time finding others who will host classes, be your own host! Pick 2 dates and plan a class in your home or at another location. Get creative with the location. Coffee shops work, but can be noisy. Parks are a great place for moms to meet while their kids play. Some libraries have rooms you can use. Look for restaurants that have back rooms you can use. Sometimes you can find a conference room or office that someone will let you use.

Personally call or text your friends. If you send an email or Facebook class invitation, make sure to follow up with a phone call or text.

Use this space to brainstorm locations for your classes.

_____
_____
_____
_____
_____
_____
_____

Teaching Tips.

Your upline leaders are committed to helping you in whatever way you need it. This means if you are not ready to teach a class, that's ok. They can help you. We have a simple process that we like to use.

1. Leader will teach the class for you & let you observe.
2. Leader teaches the class with you.
3. Leader attends and supports you as you teach the class.

Of course this is not the only way, but we have found that when someone is just getting started teaching, usually by their third or fourth class they are ready to teach themselves.

Keep your class very simple. "Make & Takes" or "Speed Oiling" classes are a lot of fun, but if your goal is to enroll people, then stick to the intro class in the beginning. The classes other than the Intro class are wonderful classes to do with your members as follow up education.

Serve very simple refreshments like Citrus water and chips with guacamole. Only set out a few products, not the whole catalog worth. You want potential builders to come & be confident they could do what you are doing. Keeping it simple is key.

We have found great success in teaching from a script. There are several reasons for this.

1. Keeps you on topic.
2. Keeps you compliant.
3. Keeps you duplicable.

Talk with your upline leader about her script. Most who are teaching on a regular basis have an outline at least for their basic intro class and love when their new builders ask to use it. If you are a Dynamic LIFE member, your leader will be happy to share her script with you. Tweak it to fit your teaching style. Enjoy this process!

© Dana Bailey, All Rights Reserved 2016

Step 4: Follow Up

Have you heard the saying, *"The fortune is in the follow up?"* It's true! Follow up is critical and for some it will take several touches by you before they finally join. I wish everyone would join the first time I show them the products, but for most that is not the case. There is a link in the resource section called, "33 Touches". It gives a basic plan for following up with prospects. If you have a routine, you are better able to stick with it and be consistent. Routines foster confidence and ultimately a degree of success.

Following up with Prospects

How do we follow up?

- Phone call or Text message,
    - "Hi there, just checking in to see if you had any questions about the class we had a few days ago?"
    - "Have you had a chance to try the samples I sent you?"
- Handwritten note. This is a lost art. Can you remember the last time you received a handwritten note in the mail from someone? It speaks volumes when we write a handwritten note to someone we have shared the oils with. We don't even have to mention oils, just let them know you are thinking about them.

Following up with New Members

Helping our new members get off to a great start is so important! We want to make sure they know we understand how overwhelming it can be getting started in something new so we are here to help. Here is a simple timeline we like to follow for our new members.

- **Day 1**: Email them a welcome letter with links to help them get to know the Young Living site and where to find reference material and information about Essential Rewards. A sample welcome letter is located in the back of this guide.
- **Day 7**: Mail them a New Member packet. Keep it simple with a few resources to help them. Ask your upline what they send out.
- **Day 10**: Call them to make sure they received their Premium Starter Kit and the New Member packet. If they haven't opened their box yet, see if they will open it while you are on the phone with them. Help them understand how to use their diffuser, put the roller fitment on the oil of their choice, etc..
- **Day 30**: Text them to see how they are enjoying their products. "*What is your favorite oil so far?*" Make sure they know how to place their next order. Begin creating dialogue with your new members.

© Dana Bailey, All Rights Reserved 2016

Step 5: Structure Your Organization

Watching your organization grow is exciting! As you continue to add new members to your organization, building strategically is important if you want to quickly move up in rank and make the most of the compensation plan. There are many different and proven ways you can structure your organization. However, there is no perfect way to do it. We learn as we go and we learn from others that have gone before us.

Remember the 7 circles of relationships you identified earlier? These will represent your seven legs. The first person you enroll in each of those circles will be on your first level in each of those legs.

As you continue to enroll friends and family, place them in the appropriate circles to create a team of people who already know and support each other. This creates a natural flow within your team. Your members are more likely to help each other when they already have things in common outside of Young Living. The Sponsor number determines where in your organization that new member will be placed.

Placing people strategically within your organization should be done with care. Watch the video link in the resources section of this guide for a simple explanation of how strategic structure can work.

© Dana Bailey, All Rights Reserved 2016

Step 6: Duplicate!

Momentum can happen quickly when you are teaching others how to get started quickly. They will share in your excitement. They will do what you do and say what you say. Be careful! It is a fact that the way you share YL with someone when they join is most likely how they will share with others. Keep things simple & basic while adding your own personal flair to your business.

Keep it Simple!

Be the example!
Keep things simple.

Use the products every day.

Talk about the products with prospects, every day.

Teach about the products every week or several times a month.

Connect people with the product every month (sign up).

Follow up. Follow up. Follow up.

Help new members get on Essential Rewards.

REPEAT.

Cycle diagram:
- Use the products everyday.
- Share the products
- Connect people with the product. (Sign-up)
- Follow up! Follow up! Follow up!
- Help new members get on ER

© Dana Bailey, All Rights Reserved 2016

Promote "4 = FREE"

Members need to:

- Sign up as a member with 100PV (PSK provides this)
- Host a class the same month
- Sign up 4 friends with a PSK
- Get at least $200 (approximately $50 per new member) in bonuses the next month. This will reimburse them for the cost of their kit

Book Classes from Classes

Have a personal goal to book at least one class at each class you have. This will help keep your calendar full and keep the momentum going. When we are able to keep regular and consistent classes scheduled we will develop a momentum among our team members that will generate a growth that once started, we just can't stop! Now that is exciting!!

Spot those Business Builders!

Young Living is a product driven company. The majority who join Young Living join because of the products. Rarely does someone join because they want to work the business side. It happens, but not very often. In fact, the majority of the Young Living leaders I know would call their business accidental. It wasn't something they pursued in the beginning, it just happened because they loved the product so much. But, it happened because their leader saw potential in them to help others and earn an income doing it.

As you are sharing, teaching, helping others get started using Young Living products, learn to recognize those who are getting involved with you. It is important that you learn to spot those potential builders. You may find when your member receives their first commission check from helping a few friends join, even though they were not previously interested in building a business, now they are interested.

So, what do we look for?

1. Look for someone who has a passion for the product. Are they living the Young Living lifestyle? Do they love learning how to incorporate the oils into their life?
2. Do they have a financial need? When my sponsor called me, she knew we had a financial need. She knew I loved the product. She knew that if she could get me past my laundry list of excuses this could work to be a blessing to us and she was right!

Learn to spot those potential business builders.

Be ready to show them how they can earn more while they share. Give them a copy of this book to help get them off to a quick and simple start. It is also a good idea to schedule a meeting with your new builders and your upline support team, whether in person of through an online meeting. This helps your new builders see what layers of leadership looks like and it will give your upline a chance to encourage and cheer on your new builders.

© Dana Bailey, All Rights Reserved 2016

*"Great things are done
by a series of small things
brought together."*
Vincent van Gogh

Step 7: Building to Silver

As momentum begins to happen within your team, duplication will begin to take over and it is a beautiful thing! Members are sharing and enrolling without you having to do anything! So, let's make sure you know now how to be strategic about building to Silver while taking advantage of all the income possibilities.

Rising Star Bonus

This bonus is based on the legs you have, their Organization Group Volume (OGV) and having the top person in each leg on Essential Rewards. Check out the video link in the resource section of this guide to better understand this fabulous bonus!

OGV: The volume (sales) of the person under you & every person under them.

ER: You and each person on your front line must have 100 PV in an ER order to qualify for this full bonus.

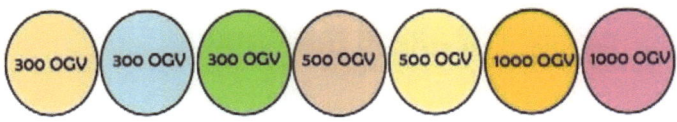

The Rising Star Bonus is often referred to as the "Diamond Maker" because it sets you up with a strong structure that can take you all the way to Royal Crown Diamond! Once your legs are at this volume, you will be at Executive.

© Dana Bailey, All Rights Reserved 2016

Focused Support

As you continue to build to Executive, you will find that specific legs could need more attention than others. Sometimes we are blessed with builders that fly on their own with little to no help from us. But, often we have a leg that needs a little help. You need 4,000 OGV total and two legs to reach 1,000 OGV in order to rank Executive so a little intentional focus on two legs will help you to reach that rank. Teach classes and offer incentives for members in that leg, make regular care calls and send notes to let those members know you are available. If you want to go beyond Executive, let's talk about what you need to do.

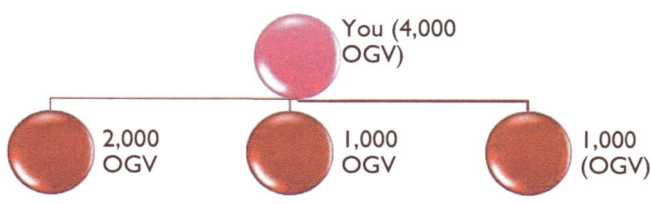

Making the Time

I'm sure you are already very busy. Many builders in YL are stay at home moms who already have a very busy schedule. It is amazing though how when we identify something important we are able to make the time for it. You will have to make time to focus on your YL business. It won't happen naturally.

Make a list of your regular activities and responsibilities. What can you keep and what can you set aside to make more available time? Some find it helpful to block off time during each day. Do what will work for you, but make your Young Living time important and protect it.

Reaching Silver & Beyond

From where you are right now, Silver may seem like a goal that is out of reach, but it is very critical that you take things one step at a time. Focus on doing the simple and basic things over and over by helping your members do the same and before you know it, Silver will not just be in reach, but it will be a reality. And if you are strategic, Gold will not be far behind.

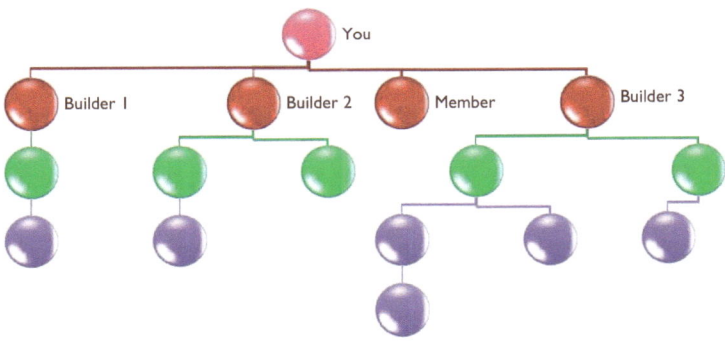

Let's think ahead.

Even though you only need 2 legs at 4,000 OGV each to reach Silver, you will need at least 2,000 more OGV, so get a third leg going strong also. You need 3 legs at 6,000 OGV each to get rank Gold, so be intentional with at least 3 of your legs.

Depending on how strategic you are as you enroll members, your organization could either have a very full first level, or go very deep. It's all up to you. If you are looking for residual income, a deep downline will provide that. If you are looking for fast money, but little residual, then a wide first level will provide that.

Set the Date!

I will reach Executive by this date: _____

I will reach Silver by this date: _____

I will reach Gold by this date: _____

I will reach Platinum by this date: _____

I will reach Diamond by this date: _____

Track Your Goals

Success can be measured. Often we don't even realize how well we are doing because we get focused on the numbers, or on our rank. It is important to write out your goals, no matter how big or small and then track when you accomplish them. It wasn't until I did this, did I realize just how much we have accomplished. As you begin to see small goals accomplished, it will motivate you to keep pushing to reach those larger goals.

"What gets measured gets done."
Jack Daly

Write your top 5 goals and the date you want to accomplish them.

Goal	Date to achieve

© Dana Bailey, All Rights Reserved 2016

Goal Planner

1. What do you want to accomplish? The end result is your goal.

2. Why is this important to you?

3. What do you need to do, or what has to happen for this goal to be accomplished?

4. How do you think you will feel once you have accomplished this goal?

List setbacks or obstacles you have faced, but also include how you have overcome them & not let them stop you from accomplishing your goal.

RESOURCES

Reference Materials & Business Building Tools

www.discoverlsp.com   www.abundanthealth4u.com
www.crowndiamondtools.com

Important Links

Rising Star Bonus:

http://www.youinfuse.com/videos/lets-talk-rising-star-bonus

Compensation 101 by YL : https://vimeo.com/106311888

Compensation video's by RCD, Monique McLean:
http://www.youinfuse.com/videos/comp

Strategic Structure by Alana Bookout ->
https://youtu.be/QfV6A7pb8Mo

Daily OGV & New Member Tracker: https://goo.gl/IteV8t

33 Touches: https://goo.gl/8tKHMo

Goal Tracker: https://goo.gl/DtKGvD

YL 2015 U.S. Income Disclosure: https://goo.gl/pqcPzL

101 Essential Oils Script: http://bit.ly/EO101script

101 Essential Oils Images: http://bit.ly/2mB3M6W

MLM Business Based

25 to Life by Adam Green
http://25tolifebook.com

Circle of Success by Monique McLean
http://shop.youinfuse.com

Driven for Success: Roadmap to the Compensation Plan by Jake Dempsey
http://www.imdrivenforsuccess.com

Road to Royal: Roadmap to Success by Debra Raybern
http://growinghealthyhomes.com/road-to-royal/

Rock Your Network Marketing Business by Sarah Robbins
http://www.sarahrobbins.com/store/rock-your-business/

GoPro by Eric Worre
http://networkmarketingpro.com/gopro/

4 Year Career - Young Living Edition by Richard Bliss Brooke
https://blissbusiness.com/Store/Products/9448.aspx

Common Abbreviations

PV: Product Value

PSK: Premium Starter Kit

OOS: Out of Stock

DL: Downline

© Dana Bailey, All Rights Reserved 2016

Daily OGV & New Member Tracker

Success can be tracked. Make it a habit of recording your daily stats from your VO. It is really handy to be able to look back and see how your organization has grown.

Find the link for a full size PDF version in the important links section.

Date	Total OGV	New Members

Sample New Member Letter

Dear Sue,

Thank you for choosing Young Living essential oils. I am one of your Care Team leaders and am available to you to help you make the most of your Young Living membership and experience.

I highly recommend you begin to get plugged into the right resources and people to help ease the feelings of being overwhelmed.

We have several Facebook groups available to our team members to help support and educate in all things Young Living. Contact the one who helped you sign up and ask them to add you to those group. You will learn so much!

Purchase reference materials. This is critical if you are serious about learning the many benefits of essential oils. One place we like to find excellent materials is: www.discoverlsp.com

Take a tour of the Young Living Virtual office. There are many resources there to help you. www.youngliving.com

We know you will love your products, so we highly recommend you consider the Essential Rewards program. You can find details in your virtual office. Contact me if you have any questions about this.

Save your sponsors number in your phone and contact her anytime you have a question or concern.

I will give you a call in a few days to make sure your starter kit has arrived and to go over the contents with you. I look forward to chatting with you. In the meantime, here is my phone number in case you have any questions.

Make your email short and simple. We don't want to overwhelm with too much information at once. Use the first month to gradually educate your new member on the basics of their membership

© Dana Bailey, All Rights Reserved 2016

Upline Contact Info

My Member #: _____ Pin # _____

Password: _____

Personal Sponsor: _____

Enroller: _____

Closest Silver leader:
_____

Facebook group: _____

Closest Gold/Platinum leader:

_____

Facebook Group: _____

Closest Diamond leader:

_____

Facebook group: _____

SOCIAL MEDIA

Facebook Pages:

https://www.facebook.com/YoungLiving/

https://www.facebook.com/yl.conduct/

https://www.facebook.com/Young-Living-Member-Services-1463191150603722/timeline

Dana's Facebook page: https://www.facebook.com/dynamiclifeYL/

© Dana Bailey, All Rights Reserved 2016

www.ingramcontent.com/pod-product-compliance
Lightning Source LLC
Chambersburg PA
CBHW041243200526
45159CB00030B/3039